Rowlands Castle and District in old picture postcards

by Peter Rogers and Paul Marshman

European Library ZALTBOMMEL/THE NETHERLANDS

GB ISBN 90 288 1131 1

Introduction

Few can question the fascination of picture postcard collecting as a hobby. These pleasing little missives bring to memory sights and scenes almost forgotten, helping one to live again through experience of holiday or travel. That the cards were placed in albums, saved or exchanged among enthusiasts, has meant that their renaissance in this current age has given the present generation an opportunity to look through the windows of the past at scenes which our parents, grandparents and even great-grandparents knew. The early photographers were keen to record anything and everything and so, perhaps unwittingly, created what is today the most comprehensive and valuable collection of photographs in the world.

Rowlands Castle attracted itinerant photographers who were prepared and able to travel to the village and its surrounds to record people, buildings and events for posterity; it is as a result of their efforts that we are able today to produce this small volume recalling times past.

Whilst the historical background of Rowlands Castle and District has been well documented over many years, the resulting written histories have yet to be advanced beyond the 'pamphlet' stage and we still await a definitive work on the subject. Neither has any previous attempt been made to publish a volume of vintage photographs, illustrative evidence to mark the passage of time in and around the village; it is with this in mind that we attempt to remedy at least part of the omission and credit the village and locality with a sense of the past.

Rowlands Castle is a village of legends, having little or no evidence to corroborate or give credence to, the folk tales concerning Rowland, said by tradition to have been a giant who preyed upon and plundered the countryside.

Early, prehistoric man created settlements in the district as is evidenced by the discovery of settled sites, flint tools and burial mounds. It is probable that it was these people who traversed the Lavant River Valley to the rich food source provided by the wildlife on the shores of Langstone Harbour. Archaeological investigations carried out in the valley give an indication that temporary, possible overnight, stops were made on what appears to have been a regular route to the sea from a 'home base' in and around the Rowlands Castle district.

The Romans, during their four hundred years or so of occupation, realised the importance of Rowlands Castle as being on the route to the local harbours from whence salt was obtained, the production of which would have provided employment and a possible source of income for the native British. Evidence of Roman influence and occupation is today common throughout the area. An abundance of brick earth was responsible for their establishing a local brick, tile and pottery industry, an industry which continued in the village until the twentieth century.

Following the Norman invasion of 1066, it is likely that camps were established in the district and small military units set up to control the native English. A series of Motte and Bailey castle fortresses were built and it is conjectured that among the several local examples, the remains which lie within the grounds of 'Deerleap House', are those of the legendary castle of Roland. Almost all of this once extensive fortress has been destroyed or removed, particularly with the coming of the railway in the nineteenth century. Here then is the probable location of the castle and we can theorise that Roland was one of the Norman King William's 'Lieutenants' who was commanded to oversee and control the district.

As a place name, the earliest reference to Rowlands Castle appears to be in the time of Edward II (1307- 1327) when there is a mention of the place, 'Rolokascastel'. In 1528, a certain John Byron was pardoned for having received cattle stolen from Rowlands Castle and in 1731, the sheriff of Havant was asked to clear gypsies from land near Rowlands Castle .

With the approaching millennium and the realisation that Rowlands Castle and its environs have provided an agreeable habitat for countless generations of our ancestors, those that are fortunate enough to reside here will appreciate the fact that they are living in what is still an enviable location. For here, on the Hampshire / West Sussex border, where time has almost past them by, a true village atmosphere still endures 'far from the maddening crowd'.

This delightful village of which its residents are justly proud, maintains its uniqueness as a designated conservation area; a thriving community within the administrative authority of East Hampshire District Council.

Acknowledgments

The fairest and simplest way to acknowledge the many sources from whence the postcards and illustrations were obtained for this volume would be collectively, to credit the villagers themselves, for it is they, who have willingly and enthusiastically, subscribed both pictorial evidence of and contributed to the knowledge of Rowlands Castle author/historian Paul Marshman. Also deserving of mention are the business men and women of Rowlands Castle , members of the Local History Society and Gavin Maidment, Senior Assistant at Havant Museum, who has expressed an interest and encouraged research into the Rowlands Castle files which are part of Local Studies and Resources facilities of Havant Museum.

1 A four-horse brake is pictured outside of the Fountain Inn in 1900. The roof line of the houses and the Railway Hotel in the background have changed but little; not so The Fountain. Later photographs show a parapet. Noticeable behind the horses are trapdoors giving access to the cellars. This side of the inn now provides staff living quarters; with the cellar entrance remaining in its original position. The bicycle is from about 1896 and would have been a much prized possession. Rowlands was a popular venue for cyclists and day trippers in the early years of the twentieth century.

2 A view of the Green dated 1901. In the centre background is the extravagantly titled 'Institute of Science, Technology and Art', a privately-funded venture to establish a school for village children not able to attend the local schools at Redhill or Idsworth. Sharing the background is the 'Chapel on the Green' built about 1880.

3 Wallis's Tea Gardens, proclaims the sign about1902, although, at this time, the pubcum tea garden was the Railway Hotel. In earlier days the name of the hostelry had been the Rowlands Castle Tavern, probably adopting the new title with the coming of the railway or, when Mr. Blake, the landlord of 1875, obtained parcel rights. Improved, enlarged and refurbished, the establishment is now renamed 'The Robin Hood '!

4 The one-time shop and general store at Durrants in 1908. The Marshall family established the business in 1841 and built up the trade to include a bakery in addition to the grocery trade. Possibly providing a post-office service (postage stamps were sold here) they also served teas and accommodated touring cyclists. Demolished in the 1960's, the modern shop premises, which later took its place, were converted into purely living accommodation in 1986.

5 St. John's Church, Redhill Rowlands Castle dated 1910, just five years after the porch was added. This photograph is of the original 'short church', the building being extended to its present length in 1929. Once again we see the legend Redhill; the ecclesiastical parish until 1953. The bold, white memorial cross marks the family grave of the Fitz-wygram family, later owners of the Leigh Park Estate.

6 Barrett's Garage about1912 when the trade appears to be concerned principally with bicycles: selling, repairing and hiring. William Barrett also specialised in oil engines. Fuelled by paraffin, these engines were the main source of power for farms, generating electricity and pumping water.

7 Mr. Barrett's Garage at Redhill about1920, cycles as well as cars providing the business. Three generations of the Barrett family are pictured with an apprentice beside a Lagonda motor car. An apocryphal tale is told of a car, similar to that in the photograph, having broken down nearby and its owner hopefully approaching 'Bill' Barrett with a damaged part to ask 'is there any chance that you could provide something similar?' 'I can do better than that,' said Bill and, after rummaging about for a short while, produced the exact part... So what was so extraordinary? The car with the problem was vintage, although the year in which this incident took place was 1990.

8 The Rowlands Castle Musical Drill Group in 1904 was led by Mr. W. Morgan assisted by his wife; they are both pictured. Each of the children here attended the Chapel on The Green Sunday School of which Mr. Morgan was superintendent.

Grace and Florence Barrett are among those children in the front row.

9 The earliest local reference to the Hall family is in 1847, when a Mr. Hall is noted as being a boot maker. A directory of 1907 then records a Henry and Edward Hall as working the business together. This would agree with the photograph which is dated 1908. These original premises with an added upper storey are still evident today, located on the sharp bend in Finchdean Road. A mainstay of the business was the manufacture of boots called 'straights'. These were, as the name implies, boots with no shape and could therefore be worn on either foot. Worn by ploughmen who constantly walked in furrows, boots became uneven in wear. With 'straights', however, the boots could be changed from foot to foot, equalling the wear, so making the boots last longer.

10 Rowlands Castle railway station. This postcard was a most welcome find, for it is the only pictorial evidence we have for the centre siding which appears on a small scale map of 1915. The siding, thought to have been provided for the excursion trade, is large enough to accommodate two coaches. There is some evidence also that horse boxes were left here and that horses destined for Goodwood Race Course were delivered to the station in the 1930's. The coaches in the background are on yet another siding which led to Courtlands Arch.

11 Rowlands Castle railway station in 1910. The London and South Western Company are operating the line, for this was before the railway amalgamation of 1922.

12 A Territorial detachment of the Royal Engineers seems to have favoured Rowlands Castle as a base for their annual camp and, in the post-card dated 5th June 1910, members of the public appear to be relaxing with the military during a break in their training routine. The field in which they are camped is today's recreation ground; the houses along Bowes Hill are still recognisable despite the fact that there are now two rows of later properties in between.

13 The Signals Co. Royal Engineers camped on the Green in 1913, recorded on a postcard with an interesting history. It was apparently written at sea aboard the Duchess of Fife en route from Southsea to Bournemouth on a day excursion, by a soldier from this camp on a day's leave.

14 The title tells all and it is only with hindsight that we know that the Great War is less than a month away. The Railway Hotel is by this time in the Brickwood's livery. The crimson tiles with white lettering were to remain until 1969. Next to the inn were stables and the entrance to the Tea Gardens. Parking on the Green is now banned and the wanton display of advertising posters discouraged!

15 'A mishap on the Green' and, once again, the Royal Engineers are involved. The photograph is a rare thing, an opportunist's snap shot reproduced as a commercial postcard. The date is sometime before 1914, for by that time the wording of the Railway Hotel had changed its style. Mr. Wallis was the landlord and the pub a Commercial and Family Hotel. Cyclists were also welcome.

16 Rowlands Castle Golf Club was formed on 6th May 1903, Admiral O'Callaghan being a keen supporter. The first club house or pavilion was apparently a converted railway coach, but this photograph shows the first permanent building. The original course was nine holes, later enlarged to eighteen holes and later again, extended to make it of championship length.

17 Despite the printed title, the building, funded mostly by public subscription, was opened in 1914 as the Parish Hall of Idsworth and North Havant, a civil parish created in 1908. The smaller (left hand) section of the building, however, had been opened in 1901 as a school exclusively for the children of Rowlands Castle and not those from Idsworth, Durrants and Redhill.

18 The Royal Engineers again, this time at a location north of the village. The point is near what are today 'Magpie Cottages', for in the background is the water tower that stood at the top of Links Lane.

19 The Green and roads became as one under the blanket of snow during the severe winter of 1916. An attempt is being made to clear a pathway for customers wishing to shop at Rook's Post Office and Stores. An enamelled sign displayed on the building advertises the fact that a public telephone is available.

20 Piped gas had been introduced into the village by 1911, although here in Woodberry Lane we see workmen installing what appear to be mains water pipes.

21 Rook's Stores and Post Office at the 'Arches' end of the village in 1920. With wide business interests in the village, the Fountain Inn was also owned by a member of the Rook family.

22 By 1937, Rook's Store had become the property of Mr. P.W. Wiggington, who later ventured into partnership with Mr. Hern; the business then became known as Wiggington and Hern.

23 Ye Little Sweet Shop, pictured with its owner Frank Burt. The shop was located by the Village Green in a spot now occupied by the Post Office. The building at the rear is the present electricity sub-station, sited here with the coming of electric power to the village in the 1930's. Many villagers can recall the days when, as children, Frank would tell them tales of his years in the Navy. They also remember the handbell, used to summon him from his home next door.

24 Royal's delivery van outside of numbers 80 to 86 Redhill Road in about 1928. The young man with his foot on the running board is Charles Royal, who would later inherit the shop and bakery on the Green. The other young man is William Farr.

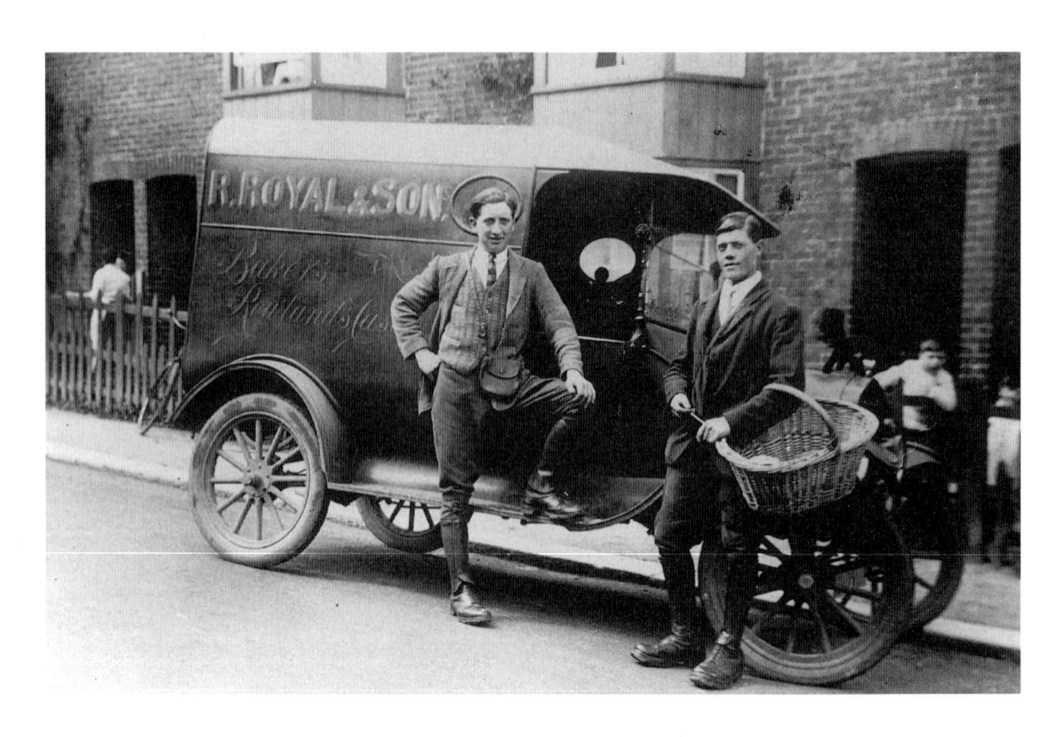

25 A view along Castle Road probably in 1912. All the houses are still there with the addition of two more which were placed on the vacant plot in 1929.

The ladies on the left of the picture have reached the road from a footpath which at this time crossed the fields, emerging at this point. Castle Road marked the old boundary between the Parishes of Havant and Idsworth and, in 1837, the limit of the ecclesiastical parish of Redhill.

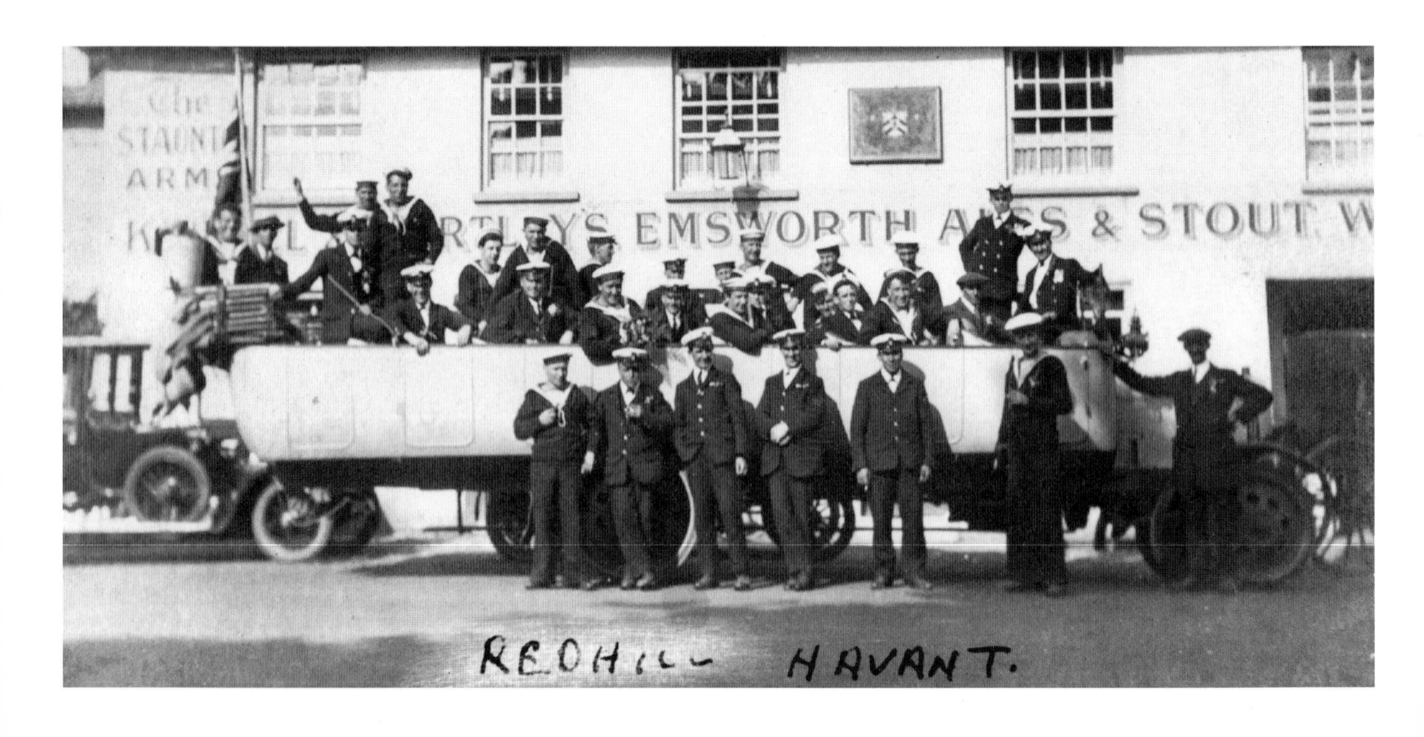

26 A postcard of the Staunton Arms which on this occasion is playing host to a visiting party of sailors. In true nautical spirit, they are flying the Union Flag from the 'after' end of the charabanc. The vehicle seems abnormally long with much of its body length behind the rear wheels. The huge concertina of a hood can be seen near the 'flagstaff'.

27 A similar, though extended view of the crossroads recorded about 1938. The public house is the Staunton Arms, so named after an earlier Leigh Park 'Squire' Sir George Staunton. The heraldic arms of the family constitute the hanging pub sign.

28 Rowlands Castle Tug of War Team 1925. Similar photographs from the same period point to the popularity of the sport. The large shield, a major trophy, now displayed in the Castle Inn, bears the names of winning teams, among them The Brickworks, Southern Railway and the Leigh Park Estate. Those team members pictured here are, from the left: T. Haskell, H. Martin, A. Wells, S. Outen, S.W. Trodd, W.R. Budd and H. Mason. In the front row: R. Knox, W. Tupper, H.M. Brigham, J. Cannings and J. Whitenstall.

29 The netball team about 1926. The minutes of the recreation ground committee refer to a Miss Thomas as being their representative. There is no record of a pitch on the playing fields, although there was apparently provision for netball at Redhill School. From left to right, the girls are: Grace Martin, Sylvia Nash, Florrie Pierpoint and in the front Eileen Haskell, Dorothy Levett and Rose Outen.

30 Durrants; more precisely, Durrants Bend as it looked in 1932. The terrace of three houses numbered 3, 4 and 5 Durrants (the numbers commencing from near the camera) were demolished about1934; the house glimpsed through the trees, however, is still there and is now numbered 72 Durrants Road. The barns on the right belonged to Durrants Farm. The origin of the name Durrants is lost in antiquity although in the past it is apparent that the settlement had been a small community in its own right.

31 The house in the photograph is known to have been built in 1905 and is one of the earliest on Bowes Hill. The event pictured is perhaps that of a gala or fête staged by members of the Nonconformist Zionist Church Movement and, whilst nothing is known of a local branch of the organisation, it may be suggested that the house, grounds and facilities were made available on the day for members who had made the journey from neighbouring towns and villages. The band providing the entertainment could be that of the Rowlands Castle British Legion or perhaps the Chalton Village Band.

32 A curious inscription appears on the reverse of the picture and reads: 'Post Office Staff and Friends at Idsworth House, entertained by Sir Dudley Clarke-Jervoise, R.T. Grey, W. Anstey and one hundred and sixteen wounded soldiers and sailors.' The year is thought to be 1916.

33 Wounded and invalid servicemen on July 17th 1916 enjoy a day trip to Rowlands Castle sponsored by the Lake Road Chapel (Portsmouth). They are pictured outside the Railway Hotel with the Fountain Inn in the background.

34 This postcard is of a garden party in the grounds of 'Deerleap', the large house that is located behind the wall bordering the Green in the centre of the village. The year is 1925 and the man walking towards the camera is Bertram Rook, a local shopkeeper. The house was, at this time , the home of the O'Callaghans, father and son, who both became admirals. Garden parties such as this were called 'at homes' and were a popular event at many large houses in the district up until the 1950's. Mr. Rook is in fact walking along an outer earthen rampart of the actual castle ruins from which the village takes its name.

35 Redhill School 1926. The photograph includes both boys and girls and suggests that, like the majority of junior schools, the classes were co-educational. The log records the fact that more than one hundred pupils were on the register in that year.

36 Inside of the Chapel on the Green. The Minister in this photograph is the Reverend Frederick Hern, the incumbent from 1901 to 1936. The lighting is by oil lamp, converted to gas in 1927. Originally having a side aisle with pews running the entire width of the building, members of the congregation complained of being unable to get in or out of their seats. The bench pews were later divided and an easier access gained from a new centre aisle. The resulting alterations have since endowed the interior with an unbalanced 'off centre' appearance.

37 Admiral O'Callaghan and his gardener Mr. Dunning are seen planting a commemorative oak tree on the village green to celebrate the Silver Jubilee of His Majesty King George V, the actual date being 6th May 1935. The ultimate fate of the oak is unknown, for the trees on the Green are now beeches.

38 The suggested scenario here at Rowlands Castle railway station is of soldiers returning to base following their summer camp. In a cheerful mood (no evidence of tearful farewells) they and a number of local lads and lasses strike a pose for the camera.

39 This delightful picture features another of the early village stores. The discerning reader may orientate him/herself, by determining that the buildings' rear left are the bungalows in Bowes Hill and that the building on the right later became a branch of Barclays Bank. Both the bank and adjoining house were demolished in 1990 to make way for the new village Surgery and Health Centre.

40 The view here is of Bowes Hill and features the newly-erected bungalows. Similar properties exist in nearby Uplands and Castle Roads. In 1930, a newspaper carried the somewhat disparaging comment that the village was rapidly becoming a Bungalow Town!

41 Redhill Cricket Team about 1912. Home games were played at Durrants in a field opposite the houses on the main road. The side probably consisted of workers from the Leigh Park Estate, changing facilities were in the local public reading room. Two of the oldest families in the area, the Outens and the Levetts, can identify their grandfathers in the photograph.

42 Redhill United Football Club played on the same ground as the cricket team of the previous picture. Within just a few years there was to be a purpose-built recreation ground at Rowlands Castle for 'the benefit of the youth of both sexes of the district'. A Durrants inhabitant expressed the opinion that 'they, the people of Durrants, would not use the ground as their own was satisfactory'. Reports of the time fail to agree and, more to the point, the lease at Durrants was due to expire!

43 The corner of the Green where it joins Links Lane. The Chapel on the Green is on the left of the scene while Rickards Tea Rooms and Gardens dominate the rest of the photograph. Rickards could provide facilities both indoors and out and were usually called upon to cater for almost all of the village functions.

44 The Village Green pictured about 1920 before it was consolidated from its original segments into the wide, uninterrupted expanse familiar to us today.

45 A view of the railway arches in about 1925 is unusual because it shows the business premises on both sides of the road. The building on the right, now a modern 'convenience store', was then owned by Mr. Hedgecock, a local builder, whose address was usually given as Finchdean, where he had another yard. On the left the shop premises are those of Mr. Rook, who features elsewhere in this book.

46 The railway arches feature once more in the Coronation celebrations of 1937. Having assembled in the Finchdean Road, the pageant led by the village band is making its way to the recreation ground, where the festivities will continue. A close examination will reveal that the clown (a lady) is smoking a cigarette.

47 Fondly referred to as the Village Band, it was in fact The British Legion Band (Rowlands Castle Branch) and shows them during a moment's relaxation during the 1935 Silver Jubilee Celebrations. From left to right are: Roy House, Erne Samsome Jr., Dennis Outen, Edward Redsull, Erne Samsome Jr., Danny Bullen, Jack Levett (just his head !), Alfred Redsull and Bill Bullen.

48 Coronation Day 1937 and the float entered by the local Dramatic Society comes to rest in front of Elizabeth Terrace on the Green. In appropriate make-up and costume, the cast are portrayed as members of the Commonwealth and British Isles.

49 Celebrations to record the ending of the war with Japan took place at Rowlands Castle Recreation Ground on September 15th 1945. A pageant of vehicles and costumed villagers having assembled here, then paraded through the village. The lorry providing a mobile display platform was owned by C. (Clarrie) Rawlings, a local coal merchant with storage facilities at the railway station and a depot at Dean Lane End. The gentleman breaking into a trot is Charlie Royal the village baker and shopkeeper. The pavilion in the background was erected in 1925 but from 1941 to 1947, was requisitioned for temporary housing.

50 This building of classic design was destroyed by over-zealous planners in 1971. Known locally as Stansted College, it was built in 1850 by Charles Dixon Esq., the then owner of Stansted House. Endowed as a charitable institution, it became a residential establishment for retired vintners, who perhaps lacked any other home or had fallen upon hard times. Keen-eyed villagers can still point out a tiny section of an original wall which remains as part of a new property.

51 A staff photograph of workers about1910. A quick head count estimates 75 men to be in the picture and, judging from their dress, they are all manual workers. Prior to the electrification of the railway, lorries could enter the works from Woodberry Lane through a pair of fine brick pillars which are still in situ today. The yard had its own railway sidings, controlled from a local signal box.

52 An interior view of the works about1925. The barrow is known as a crowding barrow and could be loaded with an average of sixty bricks; with the kiln capacities each of 90,000 bricks, it would be a long and arduous task to fill them using barrows of this type.

53 The work force had been reduced to 35 men when the brickworks finally closed in 1967. To sustain any sort of viable living, the Rowlands Castle Works in its last years was committed to producing 100,000 bricks per week. In places the complex was three storeys high with the chimney as its focal point. At a height of 150 ft it could be seen from any point in the village.

54 Located in Finchdean Road (Castle Lane of earlier years), the Castle Inn was built in 1853 when an older hostelry was demolished to make way for the railway. The Outen family were landlords for close on two hundred years, only terminating their long term tenancy shortly before the start of the Second World War.

55 The present four public houses would seem sufficient to cater for the needs of villagers and visitors alike. Prior to 1925, however, there had been a fifth, the Royal Oak at Whichers Gate Common, the last landlord being Mr. Carpenter. This photograph shows the building in 1929, when by this time it had become a farmhouse. (Mr. Pescott, the owner, is pictured standing by the fence.) The farmer's herd of cows were frequently grazed on Whichers Gate Common itself. In later years the house was divided into two dwellings and even then, occasional tricks of the light would sometimes reveal, through the limewash, the painted out name and sign of the Royal Oak. The old property was demolished and six modern houses were built there in the 1970's.

56 Titled 'Oaklands. North Havant', Oaklands House is a mid-Victorian property south of the village. It was built for Col. Stubbington, who was an avid supporter of both church and school. The description of North Havant is in fact correct for the period in which the photograph was recorded, the property was within that civil parish.

57 Idsworth House, or the New Mansion, was built from 1849 to 1851 to replace the old home of the Clarke Jervoise family; the style is mid-Victorian and the construction almost entirely of red brick. In recent years the property has been subdivided into apartments.

58 Stansted House has long had connections with Rowlands Castle although it is located just beyond the Hampshire border in West Sussex. In 1900 a disastrous fire destroyed the main building, the present, rebuilt property varying considerably from the original. This magnificent house with its extensive grounds has been the home of the Bessborough family since 1924. Descendant from an old Irish family, Vere the Ninth Earl was the first to live here. A lesser fire in 1942 destroyed the fine bijou theatre which the Earl had created in 1927.

59 The Earl was a keen supporter of the arts and his theatre was modelled on an example in London's West End. Performances were given three times each year, ranging from serious Shakespearian productions to light-hearted Christmas pantomimes. With the theatre rebuilt, a season of plays are being performed once more, particular recent favourites being the works of Gilbert & Sullivan.

60 The tiny hamlet of Dean Lane End amounts to little more than a terrace of cottages and the few houses pictured here at this minor road junction. The cottages were built by the owner of the Finchdean Iron Works to house his workers, many of the cottages still retaining the original decorative iron window frames made in those works. It was here also within this terrace at numbers 2 and 3, that the Iron Master Mr. Cannings established a school primarily for children of his employees. As his business grew, so did the school, taking in children from neighbouring Idsworth. The school closed in 1874.

61 The fickleness of the Lavant streams which occur at perplexingly uncertain intervals can still create scenes like this at Dean Lane End. Horse-drawn (and Canoe) traffic could perhaps contend with such conditions... not so the modern motor vehicles with susceptible electric components!

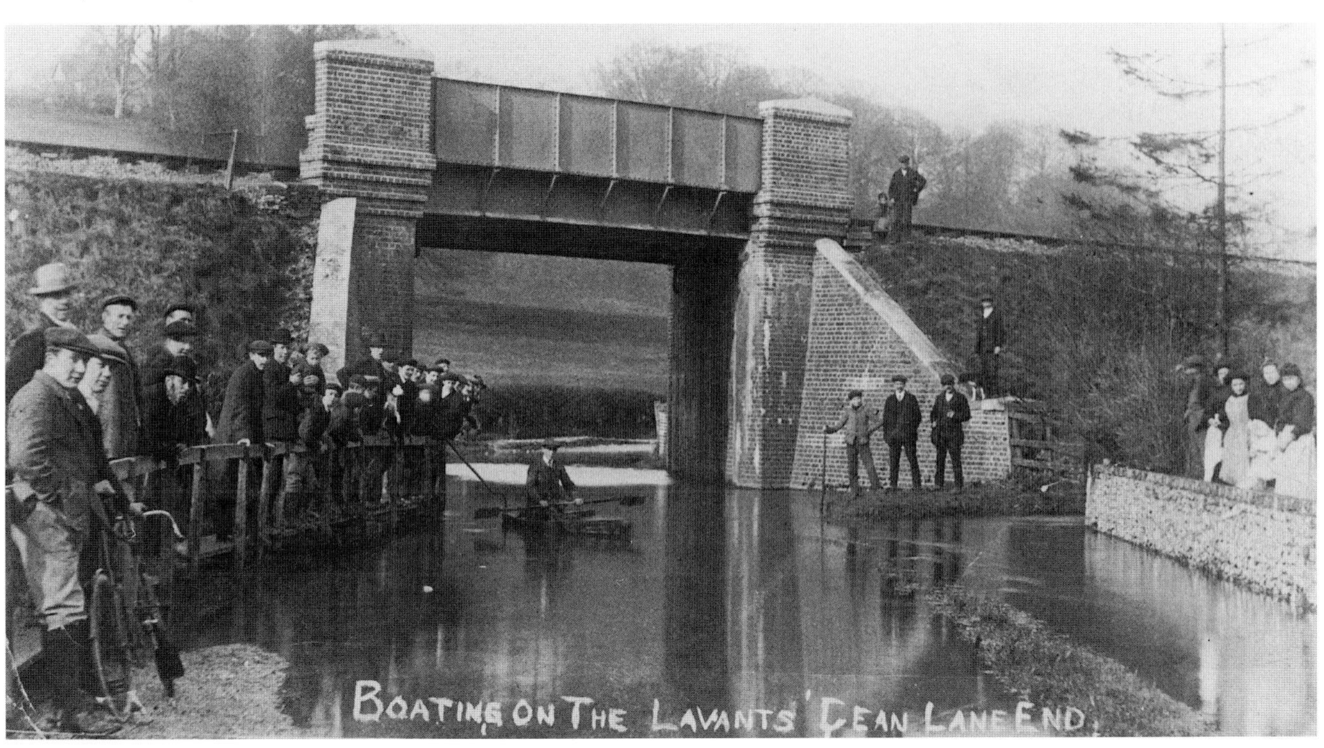

62 The view is from the small green at the heart of the community of Finchdean, representing what is possibly the earliest photograph taken in the village. The road winding away to the right leads to Wick Hanger and Chalton.

63 The blacksmith's shop at Finchdean. Each of the people in the picture are likely to be members of the local Powell family.

64 Finchdean Green about1920 showing the forge and rear of the blacksmith's shop. The partly demolished flint wall is all that remains of the Pound where stray animals could be contained until claimed.

65 Finchdean, more hamlet than village, is viewed from a local hillside in the mid-nineteen thirties. The old iron-works and the George Inn can be easily determined while, hidden among the trees, are blacksmiths' and wheel-wrights' workshops and the 'binding tree', a local peculiarity whereby metal wheel fittings etc. could be manufactured and shaped, using patterns secured to the tree itself.

66 Finchdean Ironworks, the casting shop. This interior view was recorded after production ceased in 1920. The company carried on trading, however, as suppliers and distributors to the trade.

67 Chalton is a local village much older than Rowlands Castle and, like Finchdean, has not been allowed to grow unchecked. In this postcard dated 1906, Miss Duff is standing outside the Post Office cum village store. To the rear of the shop was a bakery.

68 Chalton Benefit Band. The various styles of dress suggest that it was augmented by military personnel and perhaps members of other local bands. With village bands at Finchdean, Rowlands Castle, Horndean, Blendworth and nearby Compton, it is probable that these bands were not averse to poaching easily swayed musicians from elsewhere. A possible clue to the date is that it is pre-1914. The military men do not display World War One medal ribbons.

69 Woodcroft, never more than a farm, a farm house and a gate house for Ditcham Park, a large brick-built Victorian mansion (now a school). With the arrival of the railway, Woodcroft Farm was effectively cut in two, leaving the farm on one side and the farm house on the other side of the railway track. This footbridge was then provided and, during the last war, a small halt was constructed when Ditcham Park became a temporary naval establishment. The rail halt has been long removed and the trestle bridge replaced with a modern concrete structure that still retains the unusual, unbalanced approach ways.

70 The ancient settlement of Idsworth fails to receive attention in the Domesday Survey of 1086, although the Church of St. Hubert pictured here dates from 1053. Standing isolated on its hillside it was, nevertheless, not always so remote from any habitation. Archaeological field walks continue to yield fragments of pottery and flint from an associated Saxon settlement which had been established in the surrounding fields and aerial photographs taken when there are no crops under cultivation, reveal evidence of early building features. Occasional, seasonal risings of the Lavant water courses flood the lower levels of the fields, making church attendance almost impossible, hence the little bridge which affords dry access when necessary.

71 The stores at Forestside also served as a local Post Office. The postcard is dated 1912. The premises ceased trading in the 1960's.

72 The Robin Hood Inn at Forestside stood at the sharp bend on the road to West Marden. It was following the closure of the pub in the late 1960's that the Railway Hotel in Rowlands Castle was allowed to change its name, under new management, to the Robin Hood. The Forestside Cricket Eleven played home games in the field behind the inn.

73 Forestside Church was built in 1856 and the school in 1857, both for the newly-created Parish of Stansted and Forestside. The church is typical mid-Victorian and constructed mostly from local flint. By the time that this view was recorded, the school could support 125 pupils, although in 1910, the date of this postcard, average attendance was only 85.

FORESTSIDE CHURCH AND SCHOOL, NEAR ROWLANDS CASTLE.

74 The title is somewhat misleading as well as being misspelt (this from a photographer who was a local resident!). The building is Stansted Chapel. Parts, at least, date from the 15th century but there is more than enough evidence to suggest that the principal features are from the early 19th century only. It is for certain that a service of consecration took place on 25th January 1820, although it had been a private estate chapel since 1772.

75 It is not possible to experience this view today, trees and hedges all but shielding the houses from the road. The picture was taken in the 1930's soon after the properties were built. We are looking towards Bowes Hill; the house in the centre is Tower Cottage, so called because it was close to an old water tower mentioned elsewhere in this book. Links Lane is revealed on early maps as Dirty Lane, when it supported a farm and the tower. The suggestion is that it was renamed Links Lane because of its proximity to the golf course, or that it was the Link Road built by Clarke Jervoise for the benefit of horse-drawn carriages travelling from the station to his house.

76 Remote as Rowlands Castle was in the early days of day trippers and holiday makers, the village did not escape the attentions of the producers of comic postcards.

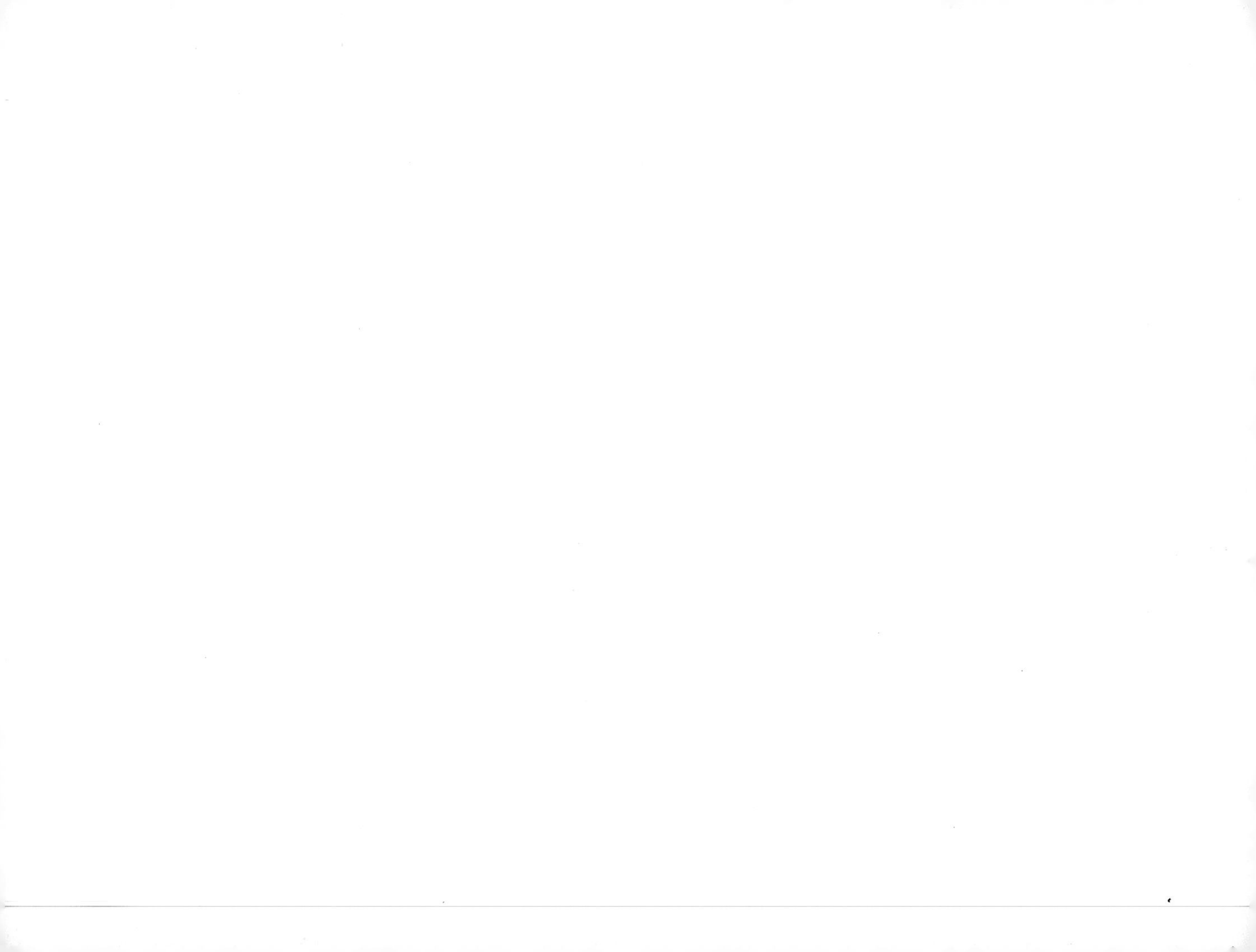